Praises From The Psalms

Eight Children's Sermons And Activity Pages

Julia E. Bland

CSS Publishing Company, Inc., Lima, Ohio

To Mary and Charles,
family musicians

ISBN: 0-7880-1767-5

Table Of Contents

Introduction And Suggestions From The Author

These lessons are taken from that great Old Testament book, the Psalms. They were originally prepared and given in the fall ending with Thanksgiving week, but praise and thanksgiving should be given all year long and these lessons can be used at any time. Although they have been prepared for use in the morning worship, they can be used at any time there is opportunity for Christian education of children.

If you are going to use the added fun in lesson eight, you might want to start now to collect empty plastic containers so that there will be enough for all the children to have a "joyful noise" maker.

* * *

Study the sermon so that you can tell it in your own words, using your own personality and with the needs of your local children in mind.

The sermon as given is to get you started. Be open to the Holy Spirit as he guides you to add your own personal observations.

If you need notes, make them small and tuck them inside your Bible at the pages where you will be reading the Scripture. Open the Bible and read from it. Children need to know that what you say really is from the Scriptures.

Ask questions and allow time for the children to answer. This will get them thinking and involved, but children can say unexpected things, so be ready to guide them back to the subject.

Before the worship hour, clip the activity sheet, a pencil, and crayons to a clipboard to be ready to hand to each child when the children's time is over.

As you pray and prepare, claim the Lord's promise in Isaiah 55:11:

So shall my word be that goes out from my mouth;
it shall not return to me empty,
but it shall accomplish that which I purpose,
and succeed in the thing for which I sent it.

Thank you for teaching our children. God will bless your efforts.

Julia E. Bland

Whole-Hearted Praise

"Praise the Lord! I will give thanks to the Lord with my whole heart ..." (Psalm 111:1a).

Scripture: Psalm 111:1; Psalm 9:1-2

Visual Aid: Paper heart with fold down the center

Handouts: Activity sheets

Advance Preparations: Copy enough activity sheets for each child to have one. Prepare your visual aid by folding an 8 x 10 or larger piece of paper and cutting it into a heart shape. (See side two of the activity sheet.) As you begin the sermon, keep the heart folded until you are ready to say, "With our *whole* heart."

The Sermon:

Today we are going to be talking about praising God. What does praise mean? When we praise someone, we are telling them they did a good job. When we praise God, we think about all that he has done and is doing. We tell about it or sing about how wonderful it all is. Then we just naturally want to thank him because we realize how much God has done for us. So praise *and* thanksgiving go together. What does Psalm 9:1-2 say?

> I will give thanks to the Lord with my whole heart; I will tell of all your wonderful deeds. I will be glad and exult in you; I will sing praise to your name, O Most High.

How does this say to praise and thank God? *(Unfold heart)* With our *whole* heart.

Have you ever heard someone say about doing a job, "My heart's not in it"? Does that mean they don't want to do the job? *(Fold heart)* Or do you clean your room halfheartedly? Does that mean you don't want to and don't do a very good job?

What would you think of a young man who says to his sweetheart, "Honey, I love you with half of my heart. Will you marry me?" She might think he's nuts. So she could answer, "I'll marry you, but my heart's not in it." That would not happen, would it? He would say, "I love you with all my heart." *(Unfold heart)* And she would say, "With my whole heart I want to marry you."

When we praise and thank God, we do it with all our hearts, not halfheartedly. What shall we praise and thank God for? *(Discuss)* We could make a very long list. We know God loves us very much to have created such a beautiful world for us to live in.

We should praise and thank him for Jesus. Jesus was never halfhearted. He loves us with all his heart. We know because he died for us.

We have so much to praise and thank God for. We'll be thinking about a few of these things in the coming weeks.

*Use visual aids

Praise God For I'm Wonderfully Made

"So God created humankind in his image ..." (Genesis 1:27a).

Scripture: Psalm 139:14; Genesis 1:27

Visual Aids: A doll made for either boys or girls

Handouts: Activity sheets

Advance Preparations: Copy enough activity sheets for each child to have one.

The Sermon:

Last week we talked about praising God. What does it mean to praise someone? We tell them they did a good job. When we praise God we talk or sing to him about the wonderful things he has done, and we praise and thank God with all our hearts.

*Look at what I brought today. Dolls are fun. We play lots of pretend games with them. Some dolls are action toys made with boys in mind. Girls seem to like baby dolls and Barbie dolls. This doll looks real, but is it alive? No. We only pretend that it is. We can make a lot of things with what God has put on our earth, but we cannot make life. Only God can create life. We will look at the book of Psalms again. Psalm 139:14:

> *I praise you, for I am fearfully and wonderfully made. Wonderful are your works; that I know very well.*

This verse praises God for making us. It says that we are wonderfully made. Have you ever thought how wonderfully God has made you? How all the parts of your body work together? The Bible tells us in Genesis 1:27 that God made us in his image. The greatest thing of all about that is that he gave us the ability to love and be loved just as he does. God loves you and me. He showed us how much when he came in Jesus to die for us. And just as we want to be loved, so does God want our love.

We are wonderfully made! Let us praise and thank God with all our hearts.

*Use visual aids

Praise God For His Word

"I treasure your word in my heart ..." (Psalm 119:11a).

Scripture: Psalm 119:7, 9, 11

Visual Aids: Bible and any of the following: scripture on tape, in Braille, in another language; Bible story book for children; daily devotion booklet; scripture on calendar or on picture to hang on wall

Handouts: Activity sheets

Advance Preparations: Copy enough activity sheets for each child to have one.

The Sermon:

We have been learning about praising and thanking God. Have you noticed that we are using the book of Psalms each time? Those who wrote the Psalms of this book in our Bible hundreds of years ago knew how to praise and thank God with their whole heart.

Today we praise and thank God for his word. *We have his word here in our Bible. People who knew and loved God wrote and kept records of what God said and did. So today we know how God loves us. We know he has plans for our future. God's word comforts us when we are sad. His word encourages us when we need help. God's word tells us when we've done wrong and that God wants to forgive us. His word tells us when we've done right. God's word gives us hope. It tells of life after death. His word tells us how to be sure of that life by trusting Jesus as Savior. God's word tells how we can live a life that is happy and good. Psalm 119:19:

> *How can young people keep their way pure? By guarding it according to your word.*

This says we guard our lives, that is, we make them good, by reading our *Bible, God's word, and living life like it tells us to.

Psalm 119 has 176 verses. They talk about God's word and how wonderful it is. We don't think much about this today, but God's word has had enemies in the past. There have been those who tried to destroy it, or at least keep it from being used. So the *Bible has come to us down through all the years kept from harm by people that were willing to die for God and his word. Today the Bible is the best selling of all books ever published.

*God's word is also on tapes to listen to and written in Braille for blind folks. It is printed for people around the world in their own language. We have God's word in Bible stories in books for children. Verses from God's word are sometimes printed on calendars or on pictures to hang on our walls, or in daily devotional books. God's word is truly loved by God's people.

Verse 7 of our Psalm says, "I will praise you with an upright heart." Why? Because of God's word. Verse 11 says, "I treasure your word in my heart."

Let us also treasure God's word. Praise and thank him for it. Read it, listen to it, as it is taught, and try hard to do as God's word has said.

*Use visual aids

Praise God For He Carries Our Burdens

"Cast all your anxiety on him, because he cares for you" (1 Peter 5:7).

Scripture: Psalm 55:22a; Psalm 68:19; Matthew 11:28; 1 Peter 5:7

Visual Aids: Some rocks in a sack; label rocks with words, such as Worried, Afraid, Guilty, Sad

Handouts: Activity sheets

Advance Preparations: Copy enough activity sheets for each child to have one. Label rocks with masking tape or tags.

The Sermon:

Do you know what a burden is? It might be something heavy to carry, such as a large bag of groceries or maybe all your toys in a box. But there is another kind of burden people carry that we cannot see. It is carried on our minds or in our hearts. It might be that we are sad or unhappy, or our feelings have been hurt. It might be that we are afraid or perhaps we've done something wrong and we feel bad or guilty.

These kinds of burdens are the hardest to carry. *Suppose you have this rock called _____. (*Give some of the children individual rocks to hold*) Now, you carry that with you everywhere. You can't put it down. It will be hard to get dressed, button buttons, and tie your shoes in the morning. It will be hard to spread jelly on your breakfast toast. It will be hard to do your work at school and hard to play any games. Remember, you can't ever put it down. You carry it everywhere. It would ruin your day, wouldn't it?

When we carry burdens like worry or fear in our hearts and minds, that too can spoil our days and perhaps our whole life.

God gave us abilities and brains. He meant that we should use them. If we are afraid because of a storm, he expects us to find proper shelter. If we are feeling guilty because we did something wrong, he expects us to say we are sorry and make things right. If we are worried about our school work, he expects us to study. But when we have problems that we cannot help, we tell God about our burdens and ask him to help. Some burdens don't go away even when we ask, but God helps us carry them. He will support, comfort, and encourage.

David, who wrote many of the Psalms, had many burdens to carry. He carried a burden of guilt, because he had done some very bad things. He carried a burden of fear, because he had enemies, and he ran away to hide from them. He carried a burden of sadness, because his own son turned against him and became his enemy. Yet through all of this, David could praise God with his whole heart. Why? Because he let God carry his burdens. In two Psalms he tells us:

> *Cast your burden on the Lord, and he will sustain you* (Psalm 55:22).

> *Blessed [or praise] be the Lord, who daily bears us up; God is our salvation* (Psalm 68:19).

Many years after the Psalms were written, Jesus came saying the same kind of thing in Matthew 11:28:

> *Come to me, all you that are weary and are carrying heavy burdens, and I will give you rest.*

So when you have problems, take them all to Jesus in your prayers. He loves you; he will help. We praise and thank him because he helps.

*Use visual aids

8

Praise God For Food

"... The earth is satisfied with the fruit of your work" (Psalm 104:13b).

Scripture: Psalm 104:13b-14; Matthew 15:36; 1 Timothy 4:4

Visual Aids: Fruit or vegetables that children like

Handouts: Activity sheets, fruits or vegetables if desired

Advance Preparations: Copy enough activity sheets for each child to have one.

The Sermon:

*What do you like to eat? Apples? Oranges? Grapes? Do you like vegetables? Carrots? Corn on the cob? How about peanut butter and jelly sandwiches?

Did you know that all these things come from a tree or plant that grows out of our earth? In fact, everything we eat depends on what our earth can provide. Psalm 104:14 says:

> *You [God] cause the grass to grow for the cattle and plants for people to use, to bring forth food from the earth....*

All of this Psalm talks about God's creation and how he has created all we need for living. After telling of the wonderful things God has made the very last verse says, "Praise the Lord!"

Yes, we should praise God for his wonderful way of providing the food we need from the earth he has created. One of the best ways to do this is what we call grace or prayer before we eat. Even Jesus, the Creator, gave a prayer of thanks before eating (see Matthew 15:36). Now, if Jesus did this, I know we should. First Timothy 4:4 says:

> *For everything created by God is good, and nothing is to be rejected, provided it is received with thanksgiving.*

Can we do this in places like a restaurant or perhaps at school? Of course! We can always stop a minute and offer our praise and thanks silently.

Sometimes boys and girls like to memorize a short prayer for each mealtime. There is one on your activity sheet. Perhaps you'd like to use it.

Here is what it says:

> *Dear Heavenly Father,*
> *We praise and thank you for this day,*
> *And for hearing us when we pray.*
> *Thank you, Father, for this food.*
> *May it help us grow strong and good. Amen.*

Let's remember to give thanks to God before we eat the food he has provided.

*Use visual aids

Praise God All Creation

"Let them praise the name of the Lord, for he commanded and they were created" (Psalm 148:5).

Scripture: Psalm 148:3, 5, 7; Psalm 19:1a

Visual Aids: A seashell or use the picture from the activity sheet

Handouts: Activity sheets, seashell if desired (they can be bought at hobby and craft stores)

Advance Preparations: Copy enough activity sheets for each child to have one.

The Sermon:

We have been talking about praising God. (You might like to review past lessons.)

Today we are talking about Psalm 148. This Psalm tells us about the wonderful things God has created, such as sun, moon, shining stars, sea creatures, animals, and much more. All of God's creation praises him. Because the sun, the moon, and the stars are so great, they tell us that our God must be very, very great to have created them. Psalm 19:1a says:

The heavens are telling [praising] the glory of God....

*Have you ever seen a seashell? There was once life within this shell. The sea has hundreds of creatures large and small. All are wonderfully made by God. Psalm 148:7 says:

Praise the Lord from the earth, you sea monsters and all deeps.

Sea creatures are great creations, but they have no voice. How can they praise God, as our verse says?

Maybe it's like this. Maybe God's creatures praise him just because they are and do what he intends. You too are God's wonderful creation. You too can praise God by doing and being what God intended. Are you all that God meant you to be? If you had no voice, you could still praise God by being the best you could be. Do healthy things; do beautiful things, loving, kind, forgiving things. This is what God intended for his people.

Did God ever intend that we be hateful or unkind? Of course not. So we praise God by our voices, but we can praise him by our good actions, too. The sea creature is and does what God intends. We too should be and do what God intended. This will praise him.

*Use visual aids

Praise God For His Love
"For your steadfast love is higher than the heavens ..." (Psalm 108:4a).

Scripture: Psalm 108:4a; Psalm 117; John 3:16

Visual Aids: A cross

Handouts: Activity sheets

Advance Preparations: Copy enough activity sheets for each child to have one.

The Sermon:
What do you think of when you see a *cross? A cross should remind us of God's love for us. Why? He came to earth in Jesus and died on a cross because he loved us.

Many places in the book of Psalms talk about God's love and how we should praise God and thank him for his love. Remember that we have been talking about praising and thanking God with our whole hearts? Let me tell you what Psalm 117 says:

> *Praise the Lord, all you nations!*
> *Extol him, all you peoples!*
> *For great is his steadfast love toward us, and the faithfulness of the Lord endures forever.*
> *Praise the Lord!*

This tells us that all nations, all people, of all colors and all languages are loved by God. This love of God is not like human love. God's love is called steadfast. Sometimes the love of people is not dependable. We find we can't count on the friendship of some. Maybe yesterday we were best friends but today they've gone to be best friends with someone else. God's love is steadfast. That means his love is always there for us.

The Bible tells us in many places that God loves us. Listen to John 3:16:

> *For God so loved the world that he gave his only Son, so that everyone who believes in him may not perish but may have eternal life.*

A *cross reminds us that God not only tells us he loves us, he has also shown us his love. He did this when he came to earth in Jesus, and lived, taught, loved, and died on a cross for us.

But, God wants something from us. He wants our love. John 3:16 says he has a gift for us if we'll believe in and love him. That gift is life with him forever as part of his family. That life is a good happy life now and forever.

Let us praise God and thank him for his steadfast love.

*Use visual aids

Praise God With Music
"I will sing to the Lord as long as I live ..." (Psalm 104:33a).

Scripture: Psalm 104:33a; Psalm 147:1; Psalm 150:3-6; Psalm 100:1-2

Visual Aids: A song book and a musical instrument

Handouts: Activity sheets

Advance Preparations: Copy enough activity sheets for each child to have one. If desired, for added fun, fill some clean, empty plastic margarine containers or other plastic jars with a few beans. Put the lids on tightly to make a rattle for each child. Toward the end of the sermon have the children sing a favorite chorus of praise and keep time with their rattles. If you have ideas for other joyful noisemakers, use them too.

The Sermon:

Do you like music? Our God must like music too. Have you ever noticed on a spring or summer morning how he fills the air with the music of his birds? And he made us able to *sing and to play *instruments, and the Bible says when we praise God, a good way to do it is with music. Listen to Psalm 147:1:

> *Praise the Lord! How good it is to sing praises to our God; for he is gracious, and a song of praise is fitting.*

This is why we have songs to sing when we come to church. We call our songs hymns. Many of our hymns are about Jesus, his love for us, and his dying on a cross for us. At Eastertime we like hymns about his resurrection. At Christmas we sing about his birth. Some hymns are about the life he helps us live; some about the life we'll have with him in heaven. But our hymns are all a way of singing praise and thanks to our God. (*You might like to name and talk about one or two favorite hymns.*)

The Bible tells us we can praise with musical instruments too. Psalm 150:3-5:

> *Praise him with trumpet sound; praise him with lute and harp! Praise him with tambourine and dance; praise him with strings and pipe! Praise him with clanging cymbals; praise him with loud clashing cymbals!*

For added fun, use the following, if desired:
Here's something else the Bible says:

> *Make a joyful noise to the Lord, all the earth. Worship the Lord with gladness; come into his presence with singing* (Psalm 100:1-2).

We are going to do that here today. We will make a joyful noise as we worship God and sing his praises. (*Pass out the rattles, instruct the children and to rattle them keeping time, and lead them in a chorus they know.*)

Boys and girls, we've been praising and thanking God from the book of the Bible called the Psalms. Can you guess how this book ends? The last verse of the last chapter says:

> *Let everything that breathes praise the Lord! Praise the Lord!*

*Use visual aids

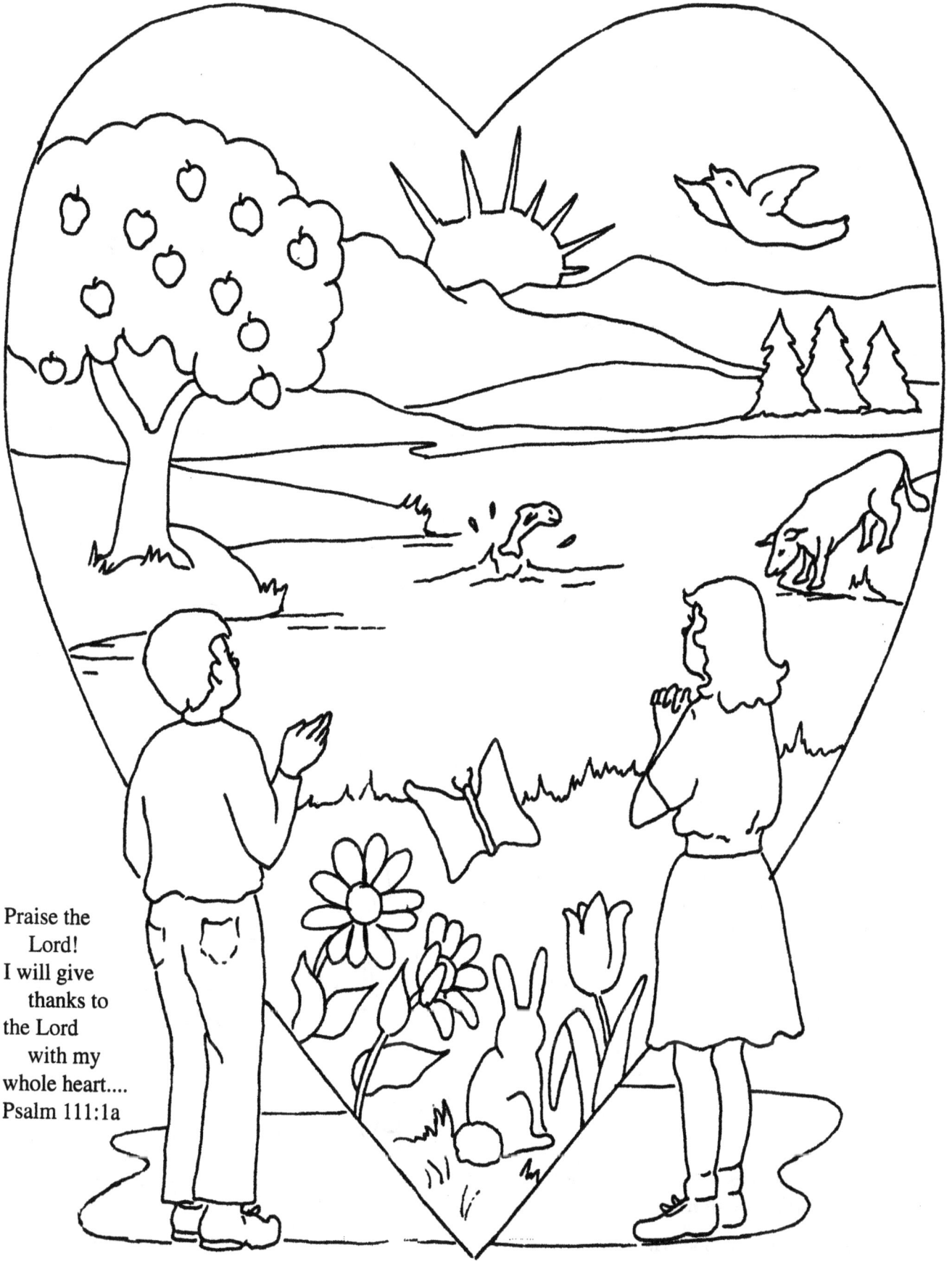

Praise the
Lord!
I will give
thanks to
the Lord
with my
whole heart....
Psalm 111:1a

It's easy to make hearts.

Fold a piece of paper.

Cut a comma shape on the

  side opposite the fold.

You can make short fat hearts,

Or tall thin ones.

Unfold for a WHOLE HEART.

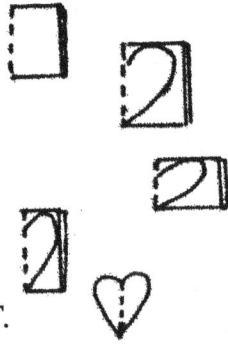

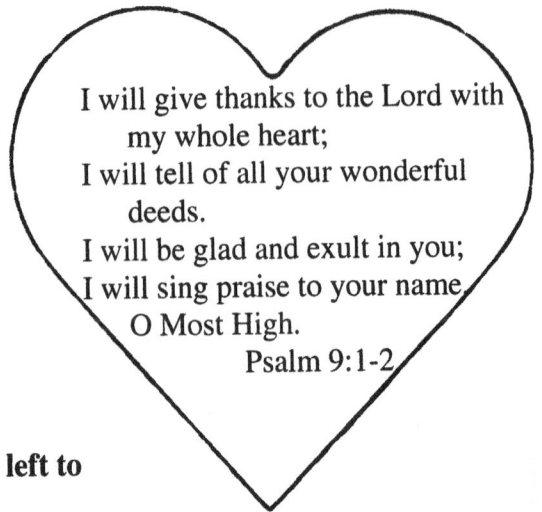

I will give thanks to the Lord with
  my whole heart;
I will tell of all your wonderful
  deeds.
I will be glad and exult in you;
I will sing praise to your name,
  O Most High.
          Psalm 9:1-2

Find words in the puzzle using words in the list. They go left to right or down.

```
W  I  T  H  D  A  Y  P  R  A  Y
H  A  L  F  H  E  A  R  T  E  D
O  H  I  S  E  S  G  A  H  V  T
L  O  R  D  A  I  L  I  E  E  H
E  X  G  M  R  N  A  S  X  R  A
M  Y  I  Y  T  G  D  E  X  Y  N
N  E  V  E  R  W  I  L  L  X  K
T  H  E  I  P  R  A  I  S  E  S
```

PRAISE	WITH	HIS
THE (2 times)	MY (2 times)	GLAD
LORD	WHOLE	PRAISES
I	HEART	EVERY
WILL	NEVER	DAY
GIVE	HALFHEARTED	PRAY
THANKS	SING	

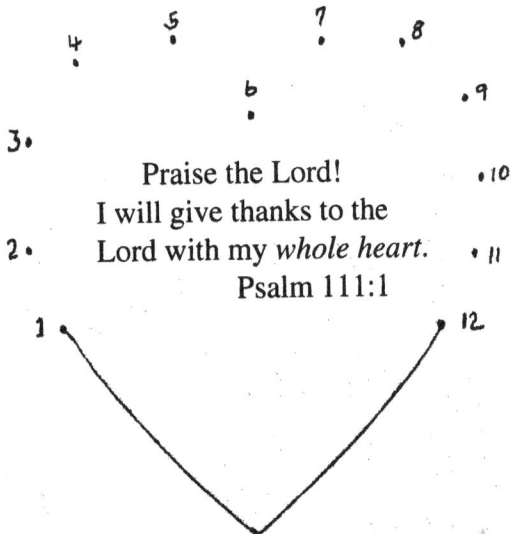

Praise the Lord!
I will give thanks to the
Lord with my *whole heart*.
      Psalm 111:1

Color the shapes marked X to find words that finish the sentence.

I praise and thank God with my

_ _ _ _ _   _ _ _ _ _!

14

I praise you, for I am fearfully and wonderfully made.
Psalm 139:14a

Find the words from the list. They go left to right or down.

```
T H A N K X F S I N G
O N L Y C R E A T E B
M A D E A X A M A D E
X X A M N P R A I S E
W O N D E R F U L L Y
G O D T H E U I I O A
I M A G E I L N F R B
L O V E O N L Y E D L
X L O V E D Y H I S E
```

PRAISE   THE   IN   TO
THANK   LORD   HIS   LOVE
SING   CAN   IMAGE   BE
GOD   CREATE   ABLE   LOVED
I   LIFE

AM (2 times)
FEARFULLY
AND
WONDERFULLY
MADE (2 times)
ONLY (2 times)

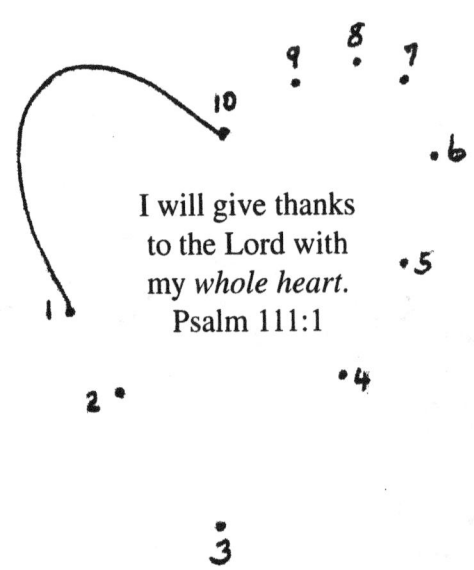

I will give thanks
to the Lord with
my *whole heart.*
Psalm 111:1

Only God could make a machine as wonderful as our bodies and give it life.

We have bones, our body's framework, giving us shape and protecting our inner parts.

We have muscles fastened to our bones. Muscles are what we use to move about. Without them we would be helpless like our doll. Our hearts and stomach are muscles too, but they are not fastened to bones.

Our heart pumps blood through our body. We must have it every minute of every day. Blood carries food, water, and oxygen to all body parts.

Our lungs pump the air we need. Our body digests the food we eat.

We have a nervous system. The brain sends messages through our nerves so that we can see and hear with wonderful eyes and ears, and so that we can taste, smell, and feel.

Skin covers our bodies protecting it, keeping it the right temperature. Our bodies grow, mend if injured, and can have babies.

Isn't God a wonderful creator!

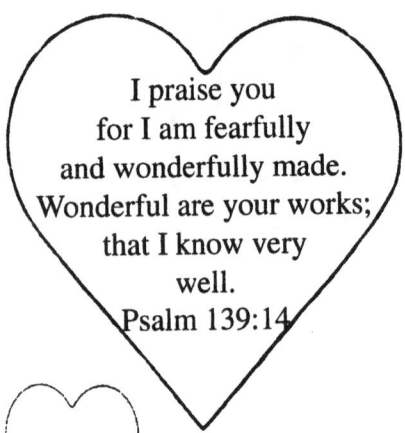

I praise you
for I am fearfully
and wonderfully made.
Wonderful are your works;
that I know very
well.
Psalm 139:14

**Color the shapes marked X
to find words that finish
the sentence.
Praise God,
I'm**

_ _ _ _ _ _ _ _ _ _ _
_ _ _ _ !

I treasure your word in my heart....
Psalm 119:11a

Find the words in the puzzle from the list. They go left to right or down.

```
E  Y  O  U  R  W  R  U  T  W  F
T  E  L  L  S  O  E  S  R  E  O
E  N  C  O  U  R  A  G  E  H  R
R  L  O  V  E  D  D  I  A  A  G
N  H  E  E  F  O  R  V  S  P  I
A  H  I  S  L  I  F  E  U  P  V
L  P  R  A  I  S  E  S  R  Y  E
C  O  M  F  O  R  T  S  E  B  S
J  E  S  U  S  U  R  E  G  I  B
T  H  A  N  K  X  U  X  O  B  O
I  N  D  C  R  O  S  S  D  L  O
H  O  P  E  F  U  T  U  R  E  K
```

PRAISE	LOVED	WE
THANK	US	TRUST
GOD	CROSS	JESUS
FOR	GIVES	LOVES
HIS	LIFE	HAPPY
SURE	SAD	ETERNAL
WORD	COMFORTS	TREASURE
IN	ENCOURAGE	READ
BOOK	FORGIVES	YOUR
TELLS	HOPE	BIBLE
HE	FUTURE	

Unscramble the words.
They are all found in the list above.

_____ and _____ God
    aserpi   ankth

for his word, the _____. It tells that
               Bbile

God _____ us and how Jesus died on a
     esvlo

_____ for us. His word _____
   ssorc   fortcoms

us if we are sad. It tells of the _____
             pphay

_____ he has for us if we trust Jesus
  tuufre

as our Savior. We will keep our _____
            feil

good if we obey his _____. God's
          drow

word is a _____.
   suretrea

7 .

6 .   With my *whole heart*
I seek you; do not
let me stray from
your commands.
5 . Psalm 119:10

4 .   . 2

. 3

Color the shapes marked X to find words that finish the sentence.

Praise God for _ _ _ _ _ _ _!

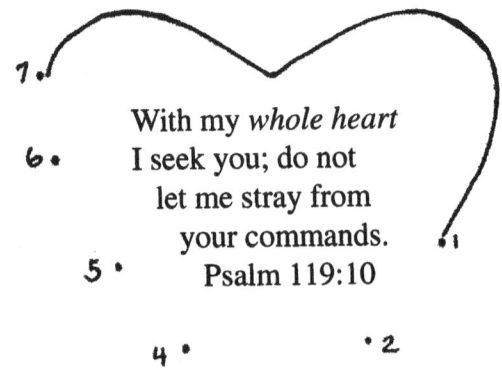

18

Cast your burden on the Lord....
Psalm 55:22a

Find the words in the list. They go left to right or down.

```
P  W  I  L  L  H  E  L  P  P
R  G  A  I  H  U  R  T  R  R
A  O  N  F  W  I  T  H  O  A
Y  D  D  E  R  U  I  N  B  I
J  F  M  I  N  D  H  O  L  S
E  E  B  U  R  D  E  N  E  E
S  E  T  O  L  O  A  D  M  W
U  L  H  E  L  O  V  E  S  H
S  I  T  A  K  E  Y  X  A  O
Y  N  A  F  R  A  I  D  D  L
O  G  U  I  L  T  Y  B  E  E
U  S  H  E  A  R  T  H  I  M
```

BURDEN	FEELINGS	WILL
HEAVY	GUILTY	HELP
LOAD	RUIN	PRAISE
ON	LIFE	HIM
MIND	TAKE	WITH
AND	PROBLEMS	WHOLE
BE	TO	HEART
SAD	GOD	JESUS
AFRAID	PRAY	LOVES
HURT	HE	YOU

Draw a line from the word to its correct meaning.

sustain   something hard to bear or endure

burden   to throw off

cast   to support, comfort, and encourage

I give thanks to you, O Lord my God, with my *whole heart.*
Psalm 86:12

Unscramble the words to find what Jesus said in Matthew 11:28.

_____ to me all _____ that are
meco   uyo

_____ and are carrying _____
ryeaw   yeavh

_____ and I will give you
dserbun

_____.
setr

Color the shapes marked X to find words that will finish the sentence.

Thank the Lord, He _ _ _ _ _ _ _ _ _ _ _ _ _ _ _ _ _ _ .

Dear Heavenly Father,
We praise and thank you
    for this day,
And for hearing us
    when we pray.
Thank you, Father,
    for this food.
May it help us grow
    strong and good. Amen.

For everything created by God is good ... provided it is received
with thanksgiving. 1 Timothy 4:4

Find the words in the puzzle from the list. They go left to right or down.

```
A  P  P  L  E  S  W  A  Y  J  P
O  R  A  N  G  E  O  S  C  E  R
E  A  T  T  H  A  N  K  A  S  O
B  E  F  O  R  E  D  E  L  U  V
C  P  R  A  I  S  E  V  L  S  I
R  L  T  H  E  T  R  E  E  S  D
E  A  T  I  N  G  F  N  D  D  I
A  N  H  F  O  R  U  W  E  I  N
T  T  I  O  Y  A  L  O  R  D  G
I  S  S  O  E  C  F  R  O  M  O
N  E  E  D  S  E  A  R  T  H  F
G  P  R  A  Y  E  R  G  O  O  D
```

THANK	WE	GRACE
PRAISE	NEED	EVEN
LORD	FROM	JESUS
FOR	THE	DID
HIS	EARTH	ASK
WONDERFUL	TREES	EAT
WAY	PLANTS	ORANGE
OF	PRAYER	APPLES
CREATING	BEFORE	YES
PROVIDING	EATING	GOOD
FOOD	CALLED	

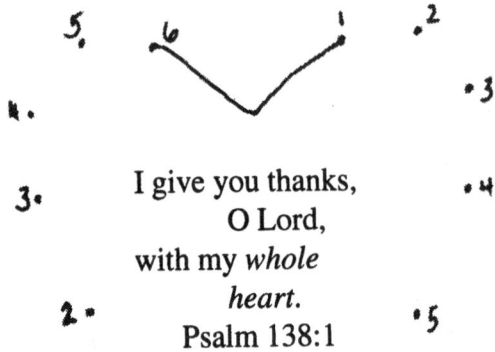

I give you thanks,
O Lord,
with my *whole
heart.*
Psalm 138:1

Color the shapes marked X to find words that finish the sentence.

Thank God _ _ _   _ _ _ _.

Unscramble the words to find what Jesus did in Matthew 15:36.

He _____ the seven _____ and the
     ootk   aloves

_____; and _____ giving _____
   shfi   retfa   anthks

he _____ them and _____ them to
      oerkb   aveg

the _____, and the disciples gave them
      disclepsi

to the _____ .
       wordcs

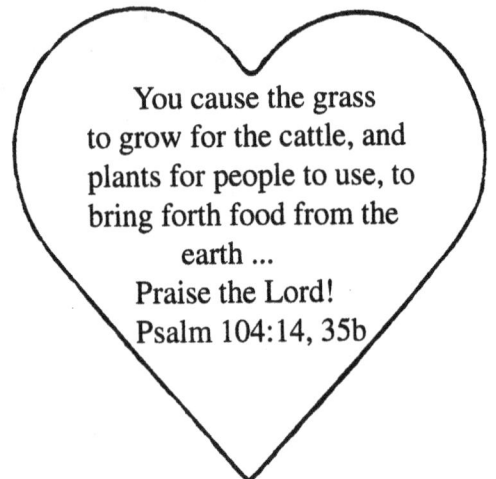

You cause the grass
to grow for the cattle, and
plants for people to use, to
bring forth food from the
earth ...
Praise the Lord!
Psalm 104:14, 35b

Sea Gull

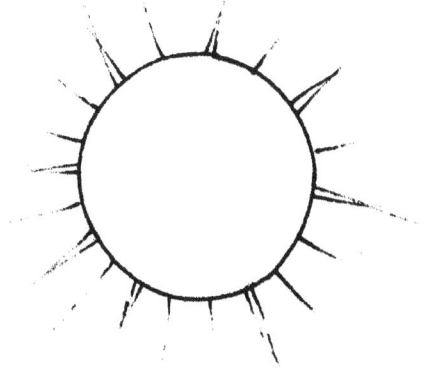

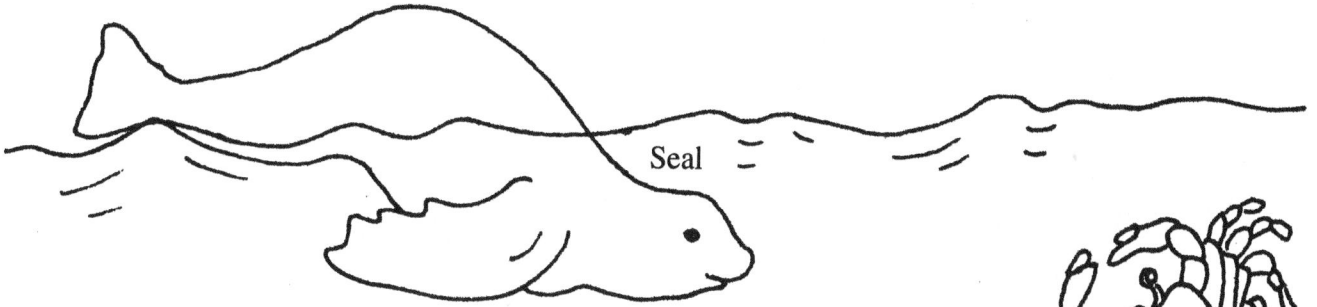

Seal

Crab

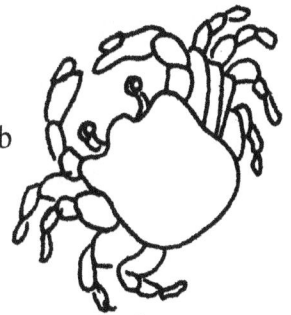

Jellyfish

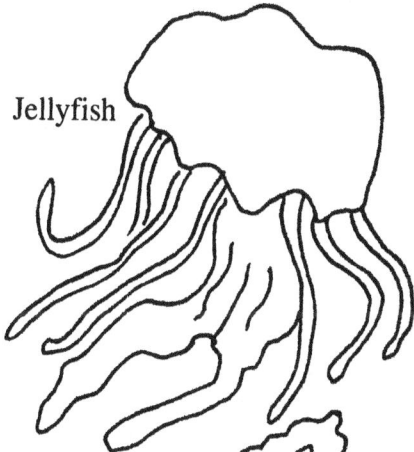

Lobster

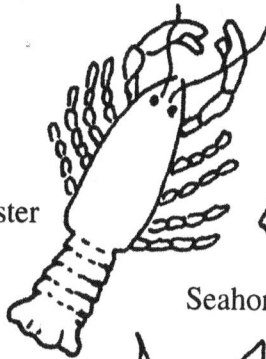

Seahorse

Seaweeds

Turban Shell

Conch Shell

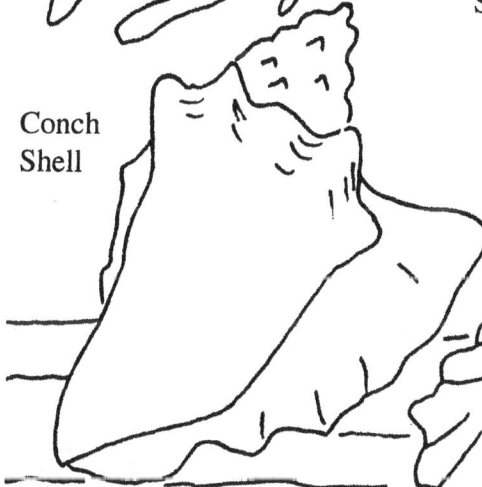

Worm Shell

Starfish

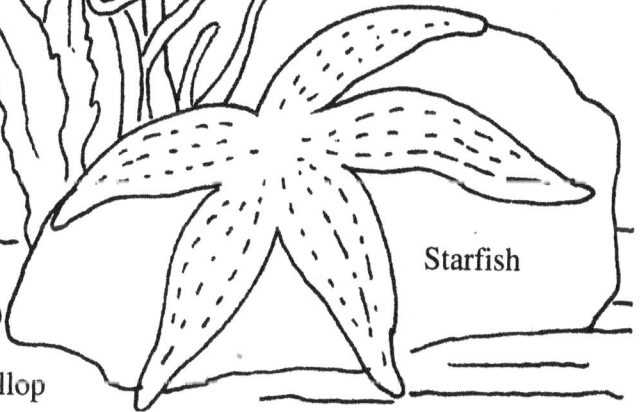

Scallop

... Praise the Lord from the heavens ... Praise the Lord from the earth, you sea monsters and all deeps.... Psalm 148:1a, 7a.

23

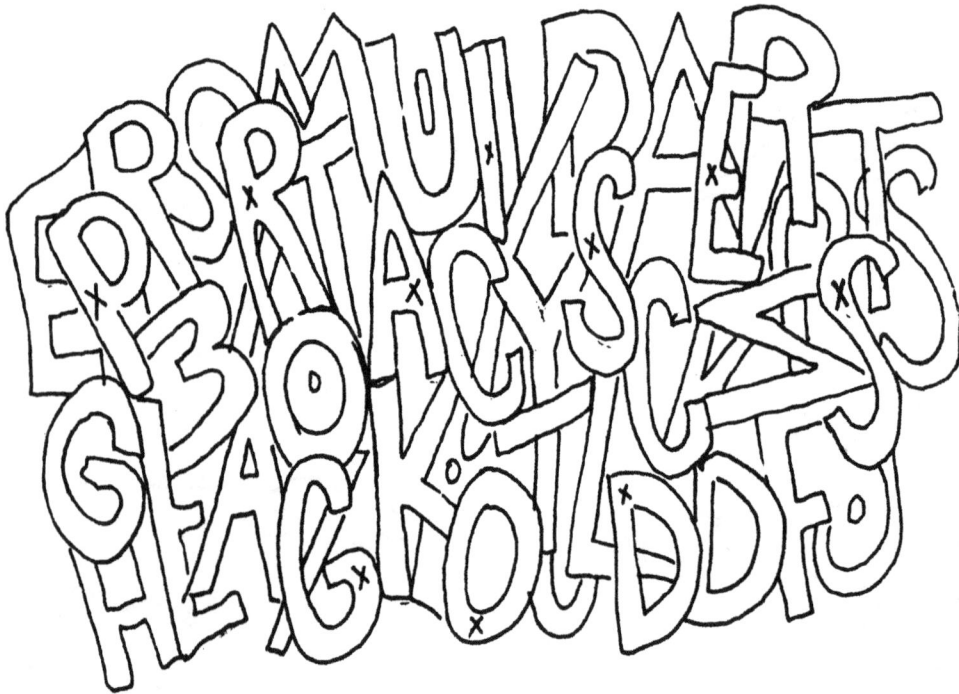

Color the shapes marked X to find words that will finish the sentence below.

All creation

_ _ _ _ _ _ _
_ _ _!

Find all the words in Psalm 148:5 in the word search puzzle. They go down or left to right.

P	R	A	I	S	E
L	O	F	C	C	X
E	X	L	O	R	D
T	H	E	M	E	A
F	W	N	M	A	N
O	E	A	A	T	D
R	R	M	N	E	A
H	E	E	D	D	B
E	T	H	E	Y	C
T	H	E	D	X	D
P	S	A	L	M	E

Let them praise the
name of the Lord,
for he commanded and
they were created.
Psalm 148:5

.5   7

4.   .8
      6
              .9
3.   I will give thanks
      to the Lord with
2•   my
        whole heart
        Psalm 9:1   10

                1•

Unscramble the words. They are from Psalm 148 found on the other side of this page.

_____ the Lord _____ the _____;
airpse   omfr   ensheav

_____ the Lord _____ the _____.
esirap   romf   rthea

24

Praise the Lord ... For great is his steadfast love toward us.
Psalm 117:1a, 2a

Work the word search puzzle using words from the list.

P	S	A	L	M	S	H	I	M	N	R
P	T	H	A	N	K	H	I	S	A	E
R	S	T	E	A	D	F	A	S	T	M
A	O	H	F	L	O	V	E	X	I	I
I	U	E	O	W	H	O	L	E	O	N
S	S	R	R	A	L	L	X	L	N	D
E	P	E	W	Y	X	C	R	O	S	S
P	R	A	I	S	E	L	O	V	E	G
X	A	R	T	E	L	L	X	E	I	O
B	Y	E	H	E	A	R	T	D	S	D

PSALMS	LOVE (2 times)
TELL	IS
PRAISE (2 times)	STEADFAST
WITH	ALWAYS
WHOLE	THERE
HEART	FOR
ALL	US
NATIONS	CROSS
ARE	REMINDS
LOVED	PRAY
BY	THANK
GOD	HIM
HIS	

Draw a line from the word to its meaning.

steadfast	endlessly or always
forever	praise
proclaim	firm, fixed and constant
faithfulness	to cry out or announce
generations	all people born year after year
extol	loyal and reliable

I give thanks to you,
O Lord my God, with
my *whole heart* ...
For great is your
steadfast love toward me....
Psalm 86:12a, 13a

Color in the shapes marked X to find words to finish the sentence.

Praise God _ _ _
_ _ _ _ _ is steadfast!

26

Praise the Lord! How good it is to sing praises to our God; for he is gracious,
and a song of praise is fitting.   Psalm 147:1

Psalm 150:3-5 mentions some musical instruments. The pictures are of those underlined. Write in the blanks what you think the name of each one is.

Praise the Lord! ... Praise him with t<u>rumpet</u> sound; praise him with <u>lute</u> and <u>harp</u>! Praise him with <u>tambourine</u> and dance; praise him with strings and <u>pipe</u>! Praise him with clanging <u>cymbals</u>; praise him with loud clashing cymbals.

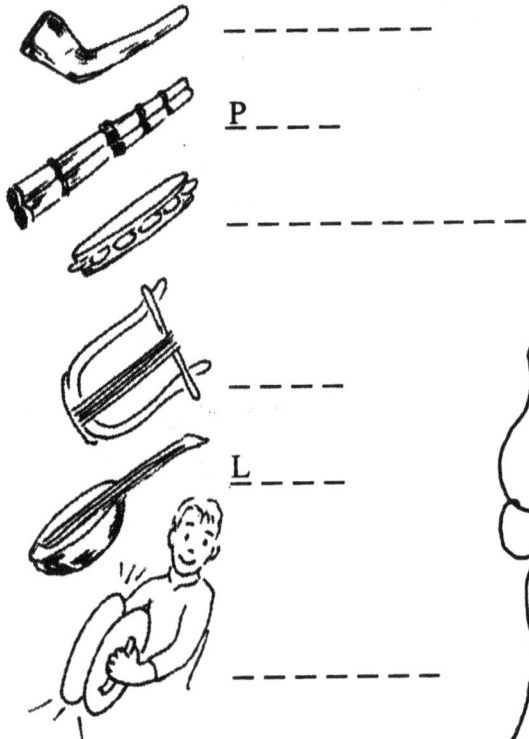

_ _ _ _ _ _ _

P_ _ _

_ _ _ _ _ _ _ _ _

_ _ _ _

L_ _ _

_ _ _ _ _ _ _

I will give thanks to the Lord with my *whole heart*; ... I will sing praise to your name, O Most High. Psalm 9:1a, 2b

Make a joyful noise to the Lord, all the earth. Worship the Lord with gladness; come into his presence with singing. Psalm 100:1-2

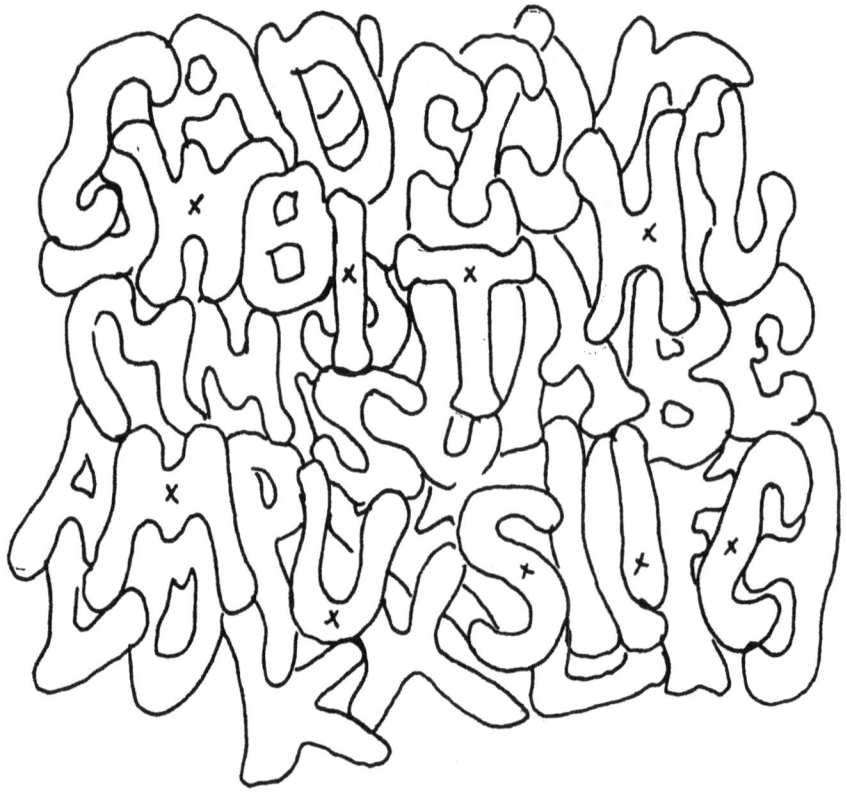

Color the shapes marked X to find words that complete the sentence.

Praise God _ _ _ _ _ _ _ _ _ _!

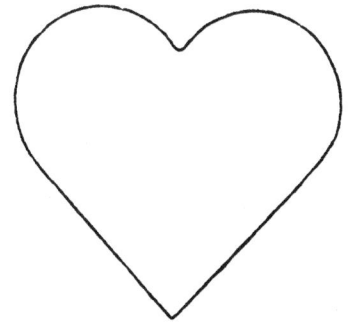

Answer Pages

Pages 14, 16

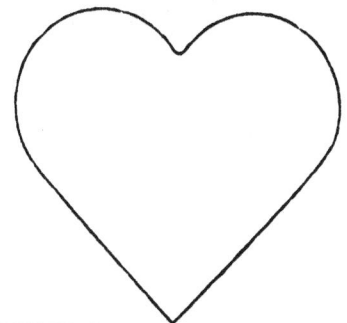

It's easy to make hearts.

Fold a piece of paper.

Cut a comma shape on the side opposite the fold.

You can make short fat hearts.

Or tall thin ones.

Unfold for a WHOLE HEART.

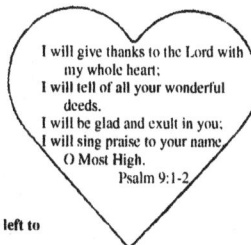

I will give thanks to the Lord with my whole heart; I will tell of all your wonderful deeds. I will be glad and exult in you; I will sing praise to your name O Most High.
Psalm 9:1-2.

Find words in the puzzle using words in the list. They go left to right or down.

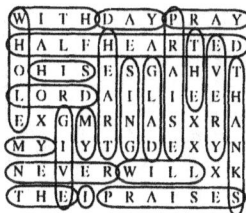

| W I T H D A Y P R A Y |
| H A L F H E A R T E D |
| O H I S E S G A H V E |
| L O R D A I L I E E H |
| E X G M R N A S X R A |
| M Y I Y T G D E X Y N |
| N E V E R W I L L X K |
| T H E I P R A I S E S |

PRAISE	WITH	HIS
THE (2 times)	MY (2 times)	GLAD
LORD	WHOLE	PRAISES
I	HEART	EVERY
WILL	NEVER	DAY
GIVE	HALFHEARTED	PRAY
THANKS	SING	

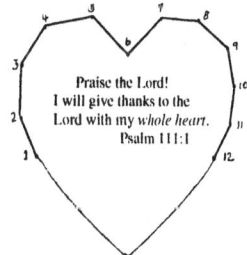

Praise the Lord! I will give thanks to the Lord with my whole heart.
Psalm 111:1

Color the shapes marked X to find words that finish the sentence.

I praise and thank God with my
w h o l e   h e a r t!

Find the words from the list. They go left to right or down.

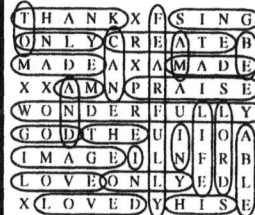

| T H A N K X F S I N G |
| O N L Y C R E A T E B |
| M A D E A X A M A D E |
| X X A M N P R A I S E |
| W O N D E R F U L L Y |
| G O D T H E U I I O A |
| I M A G E I N F R B L |
| L O V E O N L Y E D L |
| X L O V E D Y H I S E |

PRAISE	THE	IN	TO
THANK	LORD	HIS	LOVE
SING	CAN	IMAGE	BE
GOD	CREATE	ABLE	LOVED
I	LIFE		
AM (2 times)			
FEARFULLY			
AND			
WONDERFULLY			
MADE (2 times)			
ONLY (2 times)			

I will give thanks to the Lord with my whole heart.
Psalm 111:1

Only God could make a machine as wonderful as our bodies and give it life.

We have bones, our body's framework, giving us shape and protecting our inner parts.

We have muscles fastened to our bones. Muscles are what we use to move about. Without them we would be helpless like our doll. Our hearts and stomach are muscles too, but they are not fastened to bones.

Our heart pumps blood through our body. We must have it every minute of every day. Blood carries food, water, and oxygen to all body parts.

Our lungs pump the air we need. Our body digests the food we eat.

We have a nervous system. The brain sends messages through our nerves so that we can see and hear with wonderful eyes and ears, and so that we can taste, smell, and feel.

Skin covers our bodies protecting it, keeping it the right temperature. Our bodies grow, mend if injured, and can have babies.

Isn't God a wonderful creator!

I praise you for I am fearfully and wonderfully made. Wonderful are your works; that I know very well.
Psalm 139:14

Color the shapes marked X to find words that finish the sentence.
Praise God, I'm
w o n d e r f u l l y
m a d e!

29

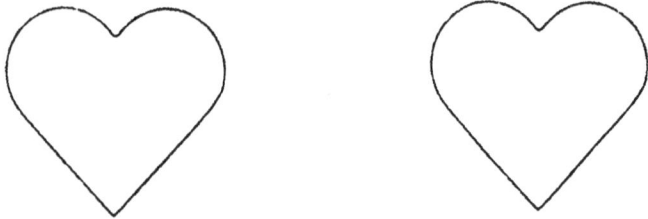

Answer Pages

Pages 18, 20, 22

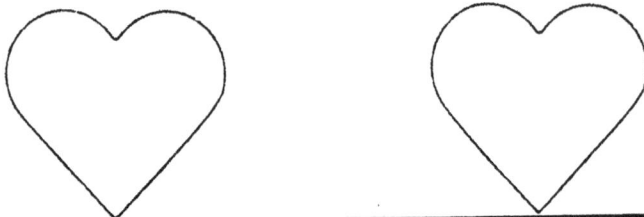

Find the words in the puzzle from the list. They go left to right or down.

```
E Y O U R W R U T W E
T E L L S O E S W F O
E N C O U R A G E H R
R L O V E D D I A A G
N H E F O R V E S P I
A H I S L I F E U P V
L P R A I S E S R Y E
C O M F O R T S E B S
J E S U S U R E G I G
T H A N K X U X O B O
I N D C R O S S O O B
H O P E F U T U R E K
```

PRAISE	LOVED	WE
THANK	US	TRUST
GOD	CROSS	JESUS
FOR	GIVES	LOVES
HIS	LIFE	HAPPY
SURE	SAD	ETERNAL
WORD	COMFORTS	TREASURE
IN	ENCOURAGE	READ
BOOK	FORGIVES	YOUR
TELLS	HOPE	BIBLE
HE	FUTURE	

Unscramble the words.
They are all found in the list above.

__Praise__ and __thank__ God
aserpi ankth

for his word, the __Bible__ . It tells that
Bbile

God __loves__ us and how Jesus died on a
esvlo

__cross__ for us. His word __comforts__
ssorc fortcoms

us if we are sad. It tells of the __happy__
pphay

__future__ he has for us if we trust Jesus
tuufre

as our Savior. We will keep our __life__
feil

good if we obey his __word__ . God's
drow

word is a __treasure__ .
suretrea

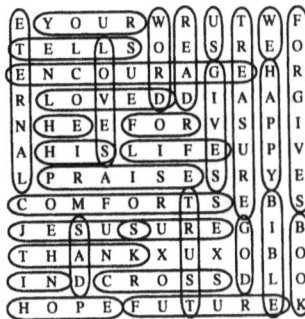

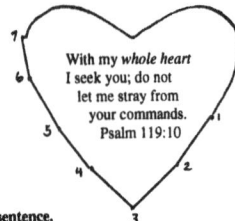

With my *whole heart*
I seek you; do not
let me stray from
your commands.
Psalm 119:10

Color the shapes marked X to find words that finish the sentence.
Praise God for __h i s__ __w o r d__

Find the words in the list. They go left to right or down.

```
P W I L L H E L P P
R A I H U R T R R A
A O N F W I T H O R
Y D D E R U I N B A
J F M I N D H O L I
E E B U R D E N E S
S L T O L O A D M E
U I H E L O V E S W
S N T A K E Y X A H
Y A F R A I D D L O
O G U I L T Y B E L
U S H E A R T H I M
```

BURDEN	FEELINGS	WILL
HEAVY	GUILTY	HELP
LOAD	RUIN	PRAISE
ON	LIFE	HIM
MIND	TAKE	WITH
AND	PROBLEMS	WHOLE
BE	TO	HEART
SAD	GOD	JESUS
AFRAID	PRAY	LOVES
HURT	HE	YOU

Draw a line from the word to its correct meaning.

sustain ─ something hard to bear or endure

burden ─ to throw off

cast ─ to support, comfort, and encourage

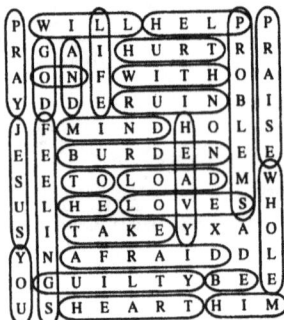

I give thanks
to you, O Lord my
God, with my
whole heart.
Psalm 86:12

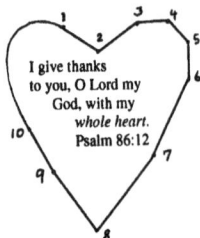

Unscramble the words to find what
Jesus said in Matthew 11:28.

__Come__ to me all __you__ that are
meco uyo

__weary__ and are carrying __heavy__
ryeaw yeavh

__burdens__ and I will give you
dserbun

__rest__ .
setr

Color the shapes marked X to find words that will finish the sentence.
Thank the Lord, He __c a r r i e s__ __o u r__ __b u r d e n s__.

Find the words in the puzzle from the list. They go left to right or down.

```
A P P L E S W A Y J P
O R A N G E O S C R R
E A T H A N K K A O O
B E F O R E D E L V V
C P R A I S E V L I I
R L T H E T R E E S D
E A T I N G F N D S I
A N H F O R U W E I N
T T I O Y A L O R D G
I O E V E F R O M
N E E D B E A R T H
G P R A Y E R G O O D
```

THANK	WE	GRACE
PRAISE	NEED	EVEN
LORD	FROM	JESUS
FOR	THE	DID
HIS	EARTH	ASK
WONDERFUL	TREES	EAT
WAY	PLANTS	ORANGE
OF	PRAYER	APPLES
CREATING	BEFORE	YES
PROVIDING	EATING	GOOD
FOOD	CALLED	

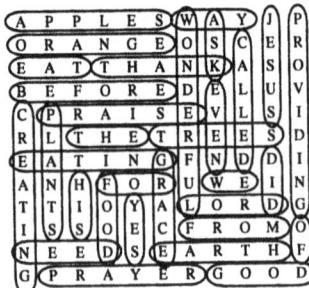

I give you thanks,
O Lord,
with my *whole
heart.*
Psalm 138:1

Color the shapes marked X to find
words that finish the sentence.

Thank God __f o r__ __f o o d__.

Unscramble the words to find what
Jesus did in Matthew 15:36.

He __took__ the seven __loaves__ and the
ootk aloves

__fish__ ; and __after__ giving __thanks__
shfi retfa anthks

he __broke__ them and __gave__ them to
oerkb aveg

the __disciples__ , and the disciples gave them
disclpsi

to the __crowds__ .
wordcs

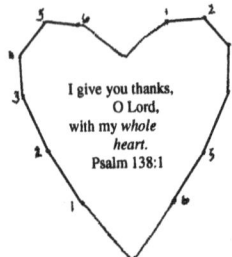

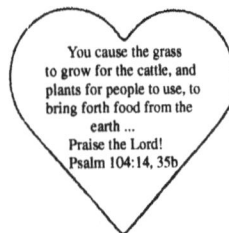

You cause the grass
to grow for the cattle, and
plants for people to use, to
bring forth food from the
earth ...
Praise the Lord!
Psalm 104:14, 35b

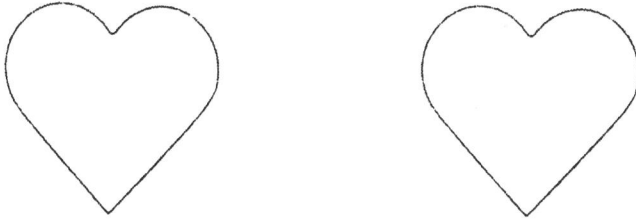

Answer Pages

Pages 24, 26, 28

Pages 24, 26, 28

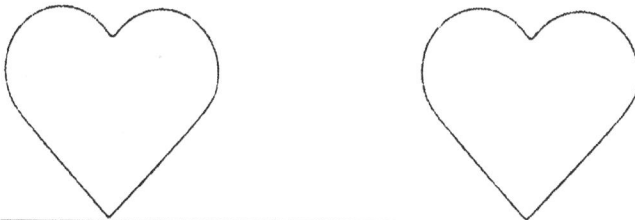

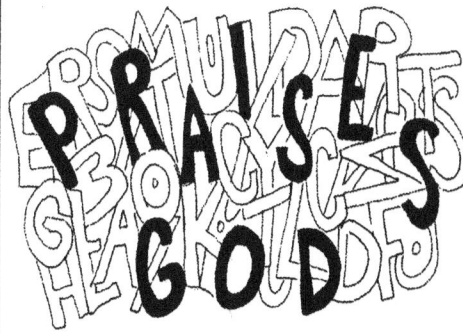

Color the shapes marked X to find words that will finish the sentence below. All creation **p r a i s e s G o d**!

PRAISES GOD

Find all the words in Psalm 148:5 in the word search puzzle. They go down or left to right.

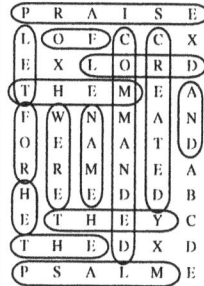

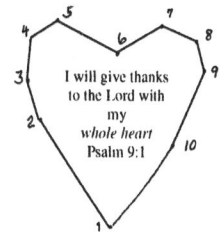

P	R	A	I	S	E
L	O	F	C	C	X
E	X	L	O	R	D
T	H	E	M	M	A
F	W	N	M	A	N
O	E	A	A	T	D
R	R	M	N	E	A
H	E	E	D	D	B
E	T	H	E	Y	C
T	H	E	D	X	D
P	S	A	L	M	E

Let them praise the name of the Lord, for he commanded and they were created. Psalm 148:5

Unscramble the words. They are from Psalm 148 found on the other side of this page.

Praise the Lord **from** the **heavens**;
airpse / omrf / ensheav

praise the Lord **from** the **earth**
esirap / roml / rthea

I will give thanks to the Lord with my *whole heart* Psalm 9:1

Work the word search puzzle using words from the list.

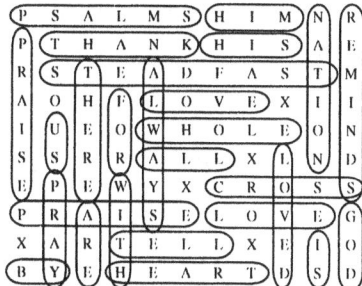

P	S	A	L	M	S	H	I	M	N	R
P	T	H	A	N	K	H	I	S	A	E
R	S	T	E	A	D	F	A	S	T	M
A	O	H	E	F	L	O	V	E	X	I
I	U	E	F	O	R	W	H	O	L	E
S	P	R	A	L	L	X	I	L	E	N
E	S	E	P	E	W	Y	X	C	R	O	S
P	R	A	I	S	E	L	O	V	E	G
X	A	R	T	E	L	L	X	E	I	S
B	Y	E	H	E	A	R	T	D	D

PSALMS
TELL
PRAISE (2 times)
WITH
WHOLE
HEART
ALL
NATIONS
ARE
LOVED
BY
GOD
HIS

LOVE (2 times)
IS
STEADFAST
ALWAYS
THERE
FOR
US
CROSS
REMINDS
PRAY
THANK
HIM

Draw a line from the word to its meaning.

steadfast — firm, fixed and constant
forever — endlessly or always
proclaim — to cry out or announce
faithfulness — loyal and reliable
generations — all people born year after year
extol — praise

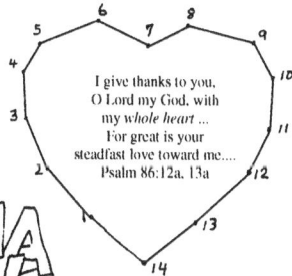

I give thanks to you, O Lord my God, with my *whole heart* ... For great is your steadfast love toward me.... Psalm 86:12a, 13a

---

Color in the shapes marked X to find words to finish the sentence.

Praise God **h i s l o v e** is steadfast!

LOVE

Psalm 150:3-5 mentions some musical instruments. The pictures are of those underlined. Write in the blanks what you think the name of each one is.

Praise the Lord! ... Praise him with t**rumpet** sound; praise him with **lute** and **harp**! Praise him with **tambourine** and dance; praise him with strings and **pipe**! Praise him with clanging **cymbals**; praise him with loud clashing cymbals.

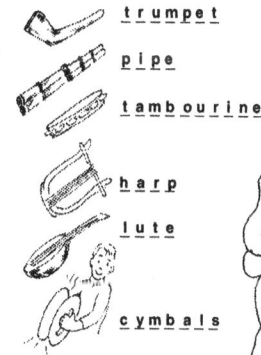

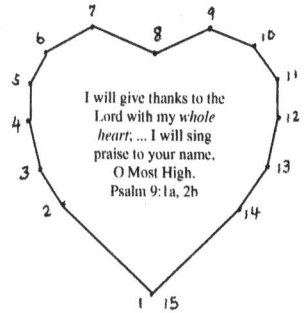

- **t r u m p e t**
- **p i p e**
- **t a m b o u r i n e**
- **h a r p**
- **l u t e**
- **c y m b a l s**

I will give thanks to the Lord with my *whole heart*; ... I will sing praise to your name, O Most High. Psalm 9:1a, 2b

---

Make a joyful noise to the Lord, all the earth. Worship the Lord with gladness; come into his presence with singing. Psalm 100:1-2

WITH MUSIC

Color the shapes marked X to find words that complete the sentence.

Praise God **w i t h m u s i c**!